Eurocommunism

A Critical Reading of Santiago Carrillo and Eurocommunist Revisionism

By: Thomas Riggins

Dubuque, IA/ Carbondale, IL USA

Winter, 2022

www.midwesternmarx.com

Midwestern Marx Publishing Press: Titles Published

1.   Thomas Riggins. *Reading the Classical Texts of Marxism*, 2022.
2.   Carlos L. Garrido. *Marxism and the Dialectical Materialist Worldview: An Anthology of Classical Marxist Texts on Dialectical Materialism*, 2022.

Some Forthcoming Titles

1.   Carlos Martinez. *No Great Wall: On the Continuities of the Chinese Revolution.*
2.   Carlos L. Garrido. *Selected Works of Henry Winston.* Prefaced by Noah Khrachvik.
3.   Thomas Riggins. *Christopher Caudwell and His Critics: A Study of Caudwell's Philosophy of Art and its Critical Responses.*
4.   Edward Liger Smith. *What About Venezuela?: How Socialism Worked in Venezuela and Why the US Needs it Too.*
5.   Yanis Iqbal. *Education in the Age of Neoliberal Dystopia.*
6.   Noah Khrachvik. *What is to be Done... Like Now?*
7.   Gabriel Rockhill, William Robinson, Salvador Rangel, Carlos L. Garrido, Edward Smith, Noah Khrachvik, Hilbourne Watson, et. al. *Against the Fake Left: A Marxist Critique of Contemporary Academic Radicalisms.*

Table of Contents

General Introduction

This article deals with the views of Santiago Carrillo (1915-2012), former general secretary of the Spanish Communist Party (1960-1982) and one of the founders of "Eurocommunism" as expressed in his book *Eurocomunismo y Estado*, translated into English as *Eurocommunism and the State* (1978).

Carrillo maintained that the conditions in Western Europe were so changed after WW2 that many of the views of Lenin and of the CPSU no longer applied to this area. Rather than simply following the line of the Soviet Union, national parties should develop Marxism according to their own history and special circumstances.

As Carrillo wrote in his introduction: "It must be recognized, however, that the approach to the problem of the State in the following pages involves a difference from Lenin's thesis of 1917 and 1918. These were applicable to Russia and theoretically to the rest of the world at that time. They are not applicable today because they have been overtaken in the circumstances of the developed capitalist countries of Western Europe. What has made them inapplicable is the change in economic structures and the objective expansion of the progressive social forces, the development of the productive forces (including nuclear energy), the advance of socialism and decolonization, and the defeat of fascism in the Second World War."

At least that is how the world looked to Carrillo in 1976. Much of this is questionable today when the economic structures have still to recover from the economic crisis initiated in 2008; the so-called expansion of the progressive social forces has called forth a revitalized ultra-right and new fascist movements; the productive forces have become responsible for the climate crisis which threatens our civilization; nuclear energy has become a threat and must be replaced wherever possible; the collapse of the Soviet Union and the east European "socialist" countries has halted any advance of socialism that Carrillo had in mind; decolonization has been replaced by neocolonialism in the guise of "globalization," and fascism seems to be having a comeback after its defeat in the Second World War. Perhaps Lenin is not as out of date as Carrillo thought.

In any event, many of Carrillo's ideas are still around today and to a greater or lesser degree have influence in Communist and socialist parties here and abroad. We shall now look at each of the six chapters of his book. I do not propose a commentary, but rather some observations based on hindsight concerning major points put forth by Carrillo in the 1970s and how well they have, or have not, withstood the test of time.

Chapter One: "The State versus Society"

Point 1.) "The capitalist state is a reality. What are its present characteristics? This is the problem of every revolution, including the one we propose to carry out by the democratic, multi-party, parliamentary road." [p.13]

In the half century since this was written there has not been one successful revolution to establish a socialist state by the means suggested by Carrillo. This is a position that has its origins in the revisionism of Eduard Bernstein and his book *Evolutionary Socialism* and all attempts to establish a socialist state by these means have been aborted. In the U.S. the ultra-right has grown and captured the Republican Party and made inroads in the Democratic Party as well. Fascist movements have grown in and outside of Europe, and within and without bourgeois democratic governments. Ministerialist, Opportunism and Pragmatism are rampant in many Communist and socialist parties and there is no real empirical evidence in support of Carrillo's ideas for a peaceful road to socialism. This doesn't mean such a road is impossible, but few parties have advanced very far along it and most have programs that actually help to perpetuate the capitalist state despite high sounding slogans and party programs giving lip service to Marxism.

Point 2.) "Socialist relations of production which rest on an insufficiently-developed basis of the productive forces can only have *formal* socialist aspects in the same sense as we refer to the *formal* freedom of bourgeois society." [p.14]

Two points are to be made here 1. Carrillo is pointing out that the Soviet Union has backward productive forces relative to the advanced capitalism of the West. 2. It has formal but not actual socialism in the same way bourgeois "democracy" is not really actually democracy but a capitalist control system to keep the working class in its place. Real democracy will only exist under socialism — real democracy doesn't exist in the Soviet Union either. This is why Communists in the West should not just follow the Soviet model. Carrillo seems to overlook the fact that his model of evolutionary socialism relies on not formal but real democracy and this undermines his peaceful road theory. The Soviet Union would eventually collapse due to – among other things – its inability to move from formal to actual socialist relations of production.

7

Point 3.) "From the *formal* Marxist point of view Kautsky was right in affirming that in Russia the conditions did not exist for achieving socialism in 1917. But the *formal* Marxism of Kautsky could not be applied to the revolutionary crisis in Russia in 1917." [p. 18]

The role of Lenin was to adapt Marxism to Russian conditions. This was a revision of original Marxism and produced Marxism-Leninism. Carrillo thus replies to his critics that his "revisionism" is no different than that of Lenin. He is adapting Marxism to the special conditions in Europe which are totally different in the 1970s than they were in Russia in 1917.

Point 4.) "Marxism is based on the concrete analysis of concrete reality. Either it is this or it is pure *ideology* (in the pejorative sense of the term) which sets reality aside and is not Marxism; and the reality of the present day in Spain, Europe and the developed capitalist world has very concrete peculiarities which we cannot avoid." [p.19]

Well, times have changed in the last fifty years. The road to socialism based on the ideals of capitalist democracy and elections has led to the possibility of a fascist takeover. Even if prevented this time around we should not deceive ourselves that this is the only, or even the best way, to think about establishing socialism.

Point 5.) "In essence, the attitude of Marx, Engels, and Lenin towards the state defines it as an instrument of the domination of one class over others, stressing particularly its coercive character. The present-day state is still the instrument of class domination defined by Marx, Engels, and Lenin; but its structures are far more complex. More contradictory, than those known to the three Marxist teachers, and its relations with society have quite different characteristics." [pp. 20, 22]

Carrillo starts with the orthodox Marxist view of the state but begins to morph into class collaboration which orthodox Marxists still believe is the road to defeat, not to socialism. The next point begins to make this clear.

Point 6.) "In the old days, the liberal bourgeois State presented the outward appearance of an *arbiter* state, which *mediated* between the opposing classes. When it intervened against the worker's protests utilizing brute force or class legislation, it did so in defense not only of one group of privileged capitalists but of all the other groups and classes of society, of principles which were challenged only by the conscious proletarian minority." [p.24]

This is not correct. It was not just the workers being oppressed by the State and everybody else being helped by it. The farmers, peasants, minorities, and small businesses were also having their interests sacrificed to the interests of the big capitalists. Marx, Engels, and Lenin were fully aware of this. Carrillo gets down to business with the next point.

Point 7.) "Conversely, the state appears today, ever more clearly, as the *director* State in all spheres, particularly that of the economy. And since it is the *director* State which no longer serves the whole of the bourgeoisie, but only that part which controls the big monopolistic groups....it is now confronted, in its capacity as such a State, not only by the advanced proletariat but also directly by the broadest social classes and strata including part of the bourgeoisie: it is entering into direct conflict with the greater part of society." [p.24]

But this is not a new phenomenon. The so-called old State also functioned this way. The main difference, Lenin pointed out, is that financial capital has replaced the older capital dominated by the big monopolies and has become

9

international so that Spain, etc., and the other developed nations are part of a globalized capitalist system dominated by the US and its junior partners the EU (AKA Germany), Japan and UK and its allies Australia, Canada, New Zealand. The class struggle has become internationalized as well. As far as the US is concerned there is no advanced proletariat (due to no CP around that wants to carry out this function) and no confrontation. Many socialists are telling the workers to support one capitalist party against the other, without explaining to them the deeper background and why they are both ultimately enemies – even when as a tactic they must sometimes support one rather than the other. This is to the right of Euro-Communism!

Point 8.) Carrillo thought that this new (really the same as the old) contradiction between the State and the various classes and strata outside of the big monopoly bourgeoise "can and must culminate in a crisis within that apparatus" I.e., the State workers come from the working and middle class and have to serve the interests of the monopoly ruling class, not their own. "It follows from this that the ideological and political currents which are developing in society have new possibilities of penetrating the State apparatus and winning important sectors of it." [p.26]

Well, in the US there is no sign that this is happening. Those on the left who try to build alliances or coalitions with the Center (an unreliable hodgepodge of conservative and liberal forces, none really progressive) find themselves increasingly irrelevant as they have played down Marxism and conceded the ideological battle ground to the Center in order not to alienate it. This blunts the developing consciousness of the workers from adopting advanced Marxist ideas and leaves them open to the neoliberal ideology of the two-party system. Nor do other advanced capitalist countries appear to have had their state apparatuses penetrated by forces hostile to their ruling class. The class struggle appears confined to the electoral arena (it occasionally breaks out in strikes, but these end with the ruling class still in control).

Point 9.) With reference to the crisis associated with capitalism, Carrillo thought these, along with "the thought-provoking actions of the vanguard forces, will undoubtedly lead to a more widespread and general understanding and to a clearer definition of the conflict between the great majority of society and the present powers of the State." [p.26]

What we have seen, however, is the growth of the ultra-right and fascist forces in Europe, and especially in the US, and a fightback led by the traditional Establishments not vanguard forces. In some areas the role of a party as a "vanguard" is played down in order to attract centrist allies (a bit of a deceit it would seem).

So much for Carrillo's first chapter. It appears as if the world did not live up to his expectations. We shall look at his next chapter in Part Two on "The Ideological Apparatuses of the State."

Chapter Two: "The Church"

Point 1.) The Church is one of the monopoly capitalist State's ideological apparatuses and in the developed capitalist world it is one of the institutions the Revolution must capture (wholly or partially). "Modern experience has shown that this is possible, and that this is the key - except in the case of war or an economic and political catastrophe, difficult to imagine today in the developed countries

11

- to the democratic transformation of the State apparatus." [p.28]

Well, this depends on the church. Some denominations have both progressive and reactionary factions, and the hierarchy will never be won over to a socialist revolution, peaceful or otherwise (the Catholic Church). There are some liberal and even progressive denominations that may be won over and some that are completely reactionary such as the US evangelicals who see Trump as sent by God to save the Republic. These churches are full of working class as well as petty bourgeois elements and some of the big bourgeois as well. We can hope that many church going people will be won over by our advanced moral positions and working class ideology but this cannot be the most important factor in the waging of the class war against the bourgeoisie, although it is an important aspect. The two exceptions, war and social catastrophe indicate that even Carrillo realized establishment religion would rally around the ruling class rather than the socialist alternative in these crises, exactly when the socialist alternative becomes necessary. As for wars being unlikely in the developed capitalist world, we only need to look at the role of NATO in the destruction of Yugoslavia and the current military operations that have broken out between Russia and Ukraine.

Point 2.) Carrillo was much more optimistic than my comment above. He thinks people motivated by their Christian faith will join the Communist Party (a secular organization based on an atheistic materialist philosophical foundation.). He wrote: "we say that with the entry of Christians, our Party has gained a new dimension; one could perhaps add that the same has happened to the faith of our Christian members. The tasks connected with material life, with social transformation, with what our cause contains of redemption, fraternity and equality, bring back to the militant Christian the evangelical values, the purity, the generous devotion of the early Christians."

These were the same Christians who, rendering unto Caesar the things that were Caesar's lined up to be fed to the lions as martyrs and as soon as they got State power spent the next thousand years warring against each other, persecuting Jews, staging crusades, and burning heretics at the stake. A Communist Party should not favor and promote one religion in the first place. Religious people should be welcome to join a CP but the CP should still adhere to its Marxist traditions which, as Carrillo himself has said, make the Church part of the ideological apparatus of the capitalist State. Religion remains the opium of the masses, although we can work with the pot smoker's segment. Trying to integrate Christians qua Christians, as opposed to working class Christians as workers into the Revolution is not likely to be successful.

Education and the Family

Point 3.) Carrillo maintained that in the universities the realization has dawned that educators are in the same relationship to the state as the working class. The educational system is in crisis and while those working and studying in it are aware the problems are caused by the system and some reforms have been enacted or proposed no real solutions to the problems of working in the system have been found.

Carrillo was certainly correct about this, except for the idea that the educational system would be moving consciously in an anti-capitalist way. The crisis is real. In the

13

US the trend is to replace full time university teachers with adjuncts, and we all know student debt is out of control. In the public school system unions are constantly fighting to maintain cost of living wages for their members and also fending off reactionary political attempts to control the curriculum. How many school boards or colleges are controlled by allies of the working class or those with socialist aims? Almost zero compared to those controlled by the right.

Point 4.) A half century ago Carrillo concluded: "Undoubtedly, the university should occupy a privileged place in the activity of the revolutionary forces." [p.35]

Well, they don't. Despite some academic Marxists and courses presenting a toothless and declawed version of Marx's critique of capitalism, the educational system is in the firm control of the ruling class. Carrillo's ideas about winning over the center and building a big coalition, even including elements of the ruling class capitalists disaffected with their monopolistic fellows, has gotten nowhere — yet many CPs and socialist parties plod along this path to nowhere, apparently unaware they are going down the road first paved by the Bernstein revisionists and latterly by the Eurocommunists. In no country in the world where the CPs or socialists have formed unity governments with centrist forces have the foundations of the ruling class and the exploitation of the proletariat been eroded or any form of genuine socialism been established. It is not solely the fault of these pseudo "popular front" Eurocommunist deviations from Marxism-Leninism but also due to the misappreciation of just how strong the world capitalist system led by the US remains even when in extreme crisis.

Point 5.) Carrillo next turned his attention to the family. The crisis of capitalism is breaking down the traditional family and its values. The alienation caused by capitalism can be seen in the development of the women's liberation movement, the freer expression of ideas by modern children revolting against their parents, and a search for a new morality. No mention is made of the sexual revolution or the gay liberation movements (ok it was 50 years ago in Catholic Spain). The family is being transformed. "The children no longer obediently follow the family's ideological traditions, as they once did: they break with them, and even influence their parents." [p.36]

Well, this is still going on. Fifty years later there have been some quantitative improvements regarding the position of women, gays, child rights, etc., but only a few years ago a president of the US was openly expressing racist, male chauvinist, anti-gay and xenophobic views in the White House, and he has built a significant movement with fanatical followers that threaten to take over large areas of the civil life and elected offices in the country. So these policies, advocated by Carrillo and his conscious or unconscious followers in the leadership of the left, have failed to pan out and have not halted the rise of and ominous growth of the ultra-right and fascist forces in the US and many other areas of the "developed capitalist world." The class consciousness of the US proletariat remains undeveloped due to the benign neglect of the AFL-CIO leadership and their left-wing political supporters who are content to pour praise on Establishment politicians who promise reforms and a fairer slice of the ruling classes' pie while ignoring the actual class struggle as explained by Marxism.

Law and Politics

Point 6.) Carrillo thought that the evolutionary socialist road he proposed would be justified by changes in the legal system. Lawyers would increasingly doubt the independence of the judicial system and its relation to the State. "[T]he opposition to traditional bourgeois justice will become more widespread." [p.37]

This fifty-year old observation is still accurate but indicates the perennial behavior of each generation with respect to the conservative nature of the law. It does not indicate that this is pointing towards the State becoming socialist. In the US progressive circles have become disgusted with the Supreme Court and the corruption of the legal system that has occurred under Trump and the Republicans but the solutions offered (e.g., political reforms, liberals being elected to Congress, expanding the Supreme Court, as well as defunding the police and reforming or abolishing the prison system) do not go beyond the horizon of maintaining the monopoly capitalist structure of the State and the existence of the market economy. The talk about socialism associated with some of these demands is purely *pro forma*.

Point 7.) While Carrillo thought the above processes were leading down the socialist road in Southern Europe (not), he was more realistic about northern (I.e., Western) Europe, what the Romans called *Gallia Transalpina*: "The block of parties and organizations that has upheld capitalism in Western Europe has been receiving encouragement, support, directives from United States imperialism, which has assumed the leadership of the capitalist world." This is a threat to democracy as it distorts the internal relations of countries subject to it." [p. 39]

This is true today as well, "Anticommunism" is directed towards China, Cuba, and other nations seeking to free themselves from US attempts to dominate and control their activities. Since it is an elementary position of Marxism that foreign policy is a reflection of domestic policy, we can see that Carrillo's remarks also pertain to the internal democratic struggles in the US. Both major parties support imperialism and undermine democracy at home — funds that people need to spend domestically on healthcare, education, infrastructure and the fight to improve the environment are drained away for the military needs of US imperialism. The democratic demands of the people for peace and improved living standards are disregarded by both major parties and fascist tendencies are forced upon the masses overtly or covertly. Carrillo was at least orthodox regarding US imperialism and Marxists know that both imperialist parties are enemies of the working people. Our movement today has to figure out how to defeat the open fascism of the Republican Party as well as the fascist warlike factions that control the Democratic Party (Biden, Pelosi, the DNC, etc.,) while at the same time supporting tactically those honest elements within the latter party which can be friendly to working class interests. In the effort to build a mass working class party many tactical policies will have to be developed over this issue to ensure that we do not fall into the ongoing revisionist trap of abandoning basic Marxist values (Webbism) and end up being duped by reactionary centrist-demands.

Point 8.) This is now moot. i.e., we have to overcome the view that our appeals to democratic values implies submitting to the views of the Soviet Union.

Point 9.) This is not moot. We must convince the people that democracy does not = capitalism. *"[D]emocracy is not only not consubstantial with capitalism, but that its defense and development require the overthrow of that*

17

social system; that in the historical conditions of today capitalism tends to reduce and in the end to destroy democracy, which is why democracy must proceed to a new dimension with a socialist regime." [p. 40]

This is an extremely important point. Marxists should not be going around spouting off about "democracy" as if it is some sort of abstract universal ideal. We should always qualify what we are talking about when we refer to the US and the struggle to preserve democracy: we are talking about "bourgeois democracy", a form of democracy created to maintain the rule of the capitalist class and the subordination of the working class. We believe in "socialist democracy," Lenin's sort of democracy, which is far superior to any form of bourgeois democracy. It is misleading to go around saying Lenin supported democracy without the qualifying context.

In the absence of socialist democracy, when the only option is bourgeois democracy or bourgeois dictatorship (fascism), then Lenin said we must fight for bourgeois democracy— but we must educate the workers about what we are doing, not go around saying Biden or Pelosi or whatever democrat is fighting for "democracy" when they're fighting for bourgeois democracy and capitalist class rule via it. The workers should also fight for it as a step towards socialist democracy (real democracy not capitalist democracy) and that it is 100% better for us and our struggle than the capitalist alternative of capitalist class dictatorship (fascism). Webbites confuse the workers by not making these distinctions and just talk about "democracy". The MAGA people do the same thing. The Webbites go around de facto defending the domestic capitalist system by defending politicians in one of its parties while claiming to oppose imperialist policies abroad— without telling the workers that imperialism abroad is the reflection of the interests of the capitalists running the system at home. Carrillo's point 9 is still valid.

Point 10.) Carrillo's point here is also valid. It is about working with other groups, even non proletarian forces, it is classic Dimitrov. We have to work with the widest class forces because the masses, the majority of the population, not just the working class per se, are being exploited by the monopolist-class strata of the bourgeoisie.

We do not work with sections of the ruling class. We may have to give critical support to a ruling class anti-fascist segment in elections, but we must also criticize them when they take anti-working class positions. They don't get a free pass. Webbites often fail to do this and say big capitalist boss X has the worker's backs, or big capitalist boss X is defending our (their) democracy, etc. It's true we may be tactically compelled to critically support big capitalist boss X, but we should explain to the masses why we do this and that he is still a big capitalist boss. We don't need to be cheerleaders for the class enemy.

Point 11.) Carrillo thought, 50 years ago, that the capitalist system was so ingrained and upheld by the labor unions and political parties that it could not be overthrown by violence, "In present conditions, the only way towards changing the ideological-political apparatus which upholds the capitalist regime is *the creation of a new correlation of forces by means of political, social and cultural struggle"* The working class must learn to speak for all segments of society exploited by the ruling class, not to just working class and union issues. "This is the precondition for assuming a hegemonic role." [p. 41]

This too is valid— other exploited segments of society can be worked with in the common cause advancing towards socialist democracy. Carrillo's use of "hegemonic" is in line with the role of Marxists being the vanguard of the revolutionary forces— not only the vanguard for the working class but of the whole mass movement for liberation. This also relates to the concept of the leading role of the party. Again, I note that Webbites do not support the idea of a hegemonic, vanguard, or leading role for the party. They seek to play a supporting role in the mass movement limiting their demands to the most advanced demands of the center — I.e., the Neoliberal consensus, creating a false impression of unity. However, on the idea of a violent overthrow of capitalism, we must say "present conditions" can rapidly change - when Carrillo wrote this the world was quite different than today. There is no longer a European socialist world, there have been two major wars in Europe (the present one in Ukraine dating from the 2014 US and NATO backed violent overthrow of the democratically elected government and the US and NATO's war in the Balkans in the 1990s to overthrow and dismember Yugoslavia, centered against Serbia.)

The Communications Media

In this section Carrillo makes two points that are still valid, one about the role of the media under capitalism and the other regarding the freedom of artistic expression.

Point 12.) "In capitalist countries, generally speaking, the media today are the most dangerous opium of the *people*." [p.43]

He means of course the role of the mainstream media (MSM) owned and controlled by capitalist corporations that twist the news to support the interests of the ruling class and its governments. The masses have little contact outside of their immediate living conditions other than what they read, see, or hear in the MSM. Now, of course, we have the Internet and all sorts of social media, but there too the capitalists control access and we have a mishmash of nonsense sites, relatively open truthful sites, propaganda sites, and individuals are at a loss as to whom to believe and trust and whom not to. By controlling information, the ruling class can keep the masses divided and off balance and less likely to challenge the system. The revolutionary forces must provide honest working class and socialist information via their own media and challenge the monopoly of information control the ruling class asserts. Today, we need an open militant Marxist press the masses can trust.

Point 13.) We must support the freedom of artistic and cultural production and work for the revolutionary forces to attain hegemony in this field. "A flourishing culture does not tolerate prohibitions and the flowering and extension of culture is the sphere in which revolutionary and progressive ideas can establish themselves, become hegemonic and have even more influence in the march of humanity, penetrating and transforming the ideological apparatuses." [p.44]

One of the fatal weaknesses of the deceased Eastern European socialist states was the attempt of the ruling parties to control and censure the arts and culture available to their people. This was the worst feature of the nanny state they created. They seem not to have trusted their own citizens and have failed to include them in the decision-making process when laws and regulations in the ideological field were drawn up.

21

The Ideological Apparatuses

This next point is still controversial. Whether it is utopian or not is controverted. Marx, Engels and Lenin (MEL) lived in a very different time than we do. They thought that the ideological apparatuses of the state (the media, education, the church, legal system, etc.,) since they were under the control of the ruling class, would have to be repressed and replaced by entirely new apparatuses controlled by the working class and dedicated to socialist construction. But times have changed. Carrillo argues that in the days of MEL it was basically just the workers and peasants versus the state, but nowadays all sorts of other strata and class formations have become alienated from the state, and they are parts of the ruling ideology. Today we can do what was not possible before. The New York Times will come out for socialism! We can appeal to these sections of the ruling classes' apparatuses and flip them. We can turn their own apparatuses against them.

Point 13.) "Certainly, one of the great historical tasks of the present time for the conquest of state power by the socialist forces is the determined, resolute, intelligent struggle to turn the weapon of ideology, the ideological apparatuses, against the classes which are in power." [p. 45]

Is this utopian? In theory it is perhaps possible, but where has it ever happened that a reigning capitalist institution was flipped while the ruling class was in power? Some may have been won over to reformism and the ruling class gradually accepted this but remained in control of the system. These systems really have to be replaced—the laws have to be rewritten, educational materials revised, etc. The position of MELS on this issue seems justified.

Developed Capitalism Bearer of Socialism

Carrillo here develops the orthodox view that capitalism has become so developed and the working class so educated in how to run it that capitalists have become superfluous as a class. MEL thought that capitalism was so productive that it was possible to eliminate poverty, hunger, homelessness, etc., and it was only that the capitalists were directing the productive forces towards private profit for themselves that prevented this. The working class could take over the system and run it themselves, not for profits but for use-values to build a classless socialist state. It would take a revolution to overthrow the capitalist dictatorship (open or masked by "democracy" rigged by them) and then a dictatorship of the proletariat (the workers in power and dismantling the ruling class power apparatuses) followed by a stateless, classless cooperative society built on humanistic foundations. Carrillo thinks, based on his previous points, we can get to that end point by peaceful means and without the need for the dictatorship of the proletariat.

Point 14.) We can bring about "the development of conditions for a new correlation of forces favorable to socialism, creating the possibility of winning and consolidating it democratically, without recourse to forms of dictatorship." [p.48] Under conditions of bourgeois democracy as are found in some advanced capitalist countries this is probably the best tactic to apply in order to build a mass party. In less developed capitalist states, we have seen

23

military coups, "color" revolutions, and US intervention used to overthrow states that have tried to use this democratic road to socialism.

Point 15.) "Just as bourgeois society was formed in the womb of the feudal regime, so socialist society has matured in the womb of developed capitalist society. This is what gives us today a material base for setting ourselves the task of turning the ideological apparatuses on which the State relies against the present class society." [p.48]

But the feudal regime's apparatuses were overthrown by wars, revolutions and the guillotine.

Chapter Three: "The Coercive Apparatus of the State"

Point 1.) Carrillo approves of the following quote from the French Communist Party philosopher Louis Althusser "So far as we know, no class can maintain state power in a lasting form without exercising at the same time its hegemony over and within the state ideological apparatuses." [p.49]

We will see below how Carrillo thinks the CP can flip these apparatuses from the bourgeois state to the support for socialism. A problem that never occurred to Carrillo when he wrote his book, and one we will not discuss, is how. without having a bourgeoisie, the Eastern European socialist states and the Soviet Union had the state apparatuses under their hegemonic control flipped over to capitalism.

Point 2.) The Soviet Union and the Russian Revolution were responses to the horrors inflicted by World War I. The Eastern European Socialist states were born out of the rubble of World War II (the defeat of the NAZIs). Wars were also the background for North Korea and China (defeat of Japanese imperialism) and Vietnam and Laos (defeat of Japanese, French, and American imperialism). This does not seem possible with respect to the developed capitalist world today as a road to socialism. A major world war today would involve nuclear weapons and the potential destruction of all the parties involved. Different roads are needed.

"They have to be roads in which democratic mass action is combined with action by the representative democratic institutions; that is to say, by the use in the service of socialism of the representative democratic instruments which today basically serve capitalism." [p.51]

Eurocommunism has, of course, failed to capture the capitalist state institutions anywhere and establish a socialist state. Nevertheless, in the developed capitalist world this is still the subtext of most all the CPs, including those which claim to reject Eurocommunism. We will now look at how Carrillo thinks we can flip the apparatuses of state monopoly capitalism to serve socialism.

Can We Democratically Capture the State Apparatus?

Fifty years ago, Carrillo detected the beginnings of a movement in the masses that would allow for the democratic takeover of the state apparatus. Social democrats were getting elected, the Dutch troops in NATO were being unionized, and the French uprising in 1968 raised the consciousness of the masses and opened the way for a socialist road to transform the capitalist state by flipping some of the capitalist state apparatuses. Centered in Paris in May 1968, seven weeks of nationwide protests convulsed France. President de Gaulle fled to West Germany, the government was paralyzed, the police refused to intervene when the students and workers marched through Paris where 50,000 marchers were expected, and 500,000 turned up. The French Communists turned out in support of demands for radical change, the army was put on alert as revolutionary ideas did not penetrate the officer corps but the troops were of the same age as the students and young workers. The Communists were thought to be about to seize government buildings and a revolution would break out: de Gaulle broadcast to the nation that a new election would be held for the National Assembly —violence should be avoided. The Communists believed in a peaceful democratic revolution and agreed to de Gaulle's plans— the workers returned to their factories; the revolt was over.

Point 3.) "This is a process which is only beginning, is therefore only incipient, and could still be diverted and manipulated by the ruling classes. It is an open question that has not been solved. It is a possible road for proceeding to the democratization of the state apparatuses as the first step towards its transformation and conversion into one capable of serving a democratic and socialist society." [p.54]

Half a century has passed and no uprising such as 1968 Paris has occurred in any of the developed capitalist countries. The ruling capitalist class is as strong and powerful as ever. Perhaps Carrillo's question about capturing the capitalist state's apparatuses by peaceful democratic means is no longer open and has been solved.

Democratization of the State Apparatus

To go down this road to socialism we will have to change our attitudes about the state apparatuses. Heretofore Marxists have seen the different arms of the state as hostile class forces, especially the police and the military, but also the prison system, education system, churches, etc. They were all tools of the class enemy that must be fought, overcome, and replaced with new proletarian versions. Instead of treating them as hostile enemies the revolution must try to democratize them and win them over to the proletarian world view. Workers in these sectors also have problems and are abused by the ruling class even as they are mobilized against the interests of the people. We must work with them, recognize their special problems, and win them over to the revolution. Instead of defunding the police we should advocate redirection of the funds towards better training and working with the people and demand the police not be used to break up strikes or to harass working people, immigrants, etc. We will find allies within these organizations and must struggle to flip them from subservience to the ruling class to a pro people democratic front with them. The Police Benevolent Society and Black Lives Matter marching together! Eurocommunists have their tasks cut out for them.

Point 4.) "It is a difficult change to make ["the man in blue is a friend to me and you" and not "a gun toting racist pig"- tr]. But it must be made, starting from the principle that in a democratic socialist society it will still be necessary to have functionaries who are specialists in the pursuit of crime, and in safeguarding the security of the population." [p. 57]

Point 5.) "The army is, without doubt, the most important of the coercive instruments of the state." [p. 57]

Carrillo discusses the role of the army throughout history as a force used to protect the ruling classes, the nobility and later the new bourgeois class after it came to power. Through two world wars it was associated with national defense (or aggression) and people thought of their army as primarily a national army defending them from foreign attacks. Most Americans still feel that way, I think, about the US Army the armed forces in general) and so did most Europeans after WWII. But something has changed, at least in Europe, and that is the development of an international force by the North Atlantic Treaty Organization, I.e., NATO. NATO was created to deter a Soviet Attack. There was never a Soviet attack. The Soviets created the Warsaw Pact to deter NATO. The Warsaw Pact was also used to prevent any of its members from deviating too far from Soviet policies. In Carrillo's day these two military blocks faced off in Europe. NATO was actually an international armed force run by the Americans. Most Europeans, he said, no longer looked on "their" national army in primarily nationalistic terms. This gives the revolutionaries an opportunity to win over the NATO officers to a peaceful socialist transition as they now have an international outlook rather than a narrow national one. The implication for Spain was that the Spanish army would not intervene to defend a ruling class that lost an election to the revolutionary forces. This would also be the case in other NATO countries.

But this view of Carrillo's is contradicted by Point 6.) "In the last resort [NATO] remains above all an instrument of American political, economic and military control over Europe." [p.60]

The Americans would use NATO to intervene in any European country so unwise as to elect a communist government. What has happened in the 50 years since Carrillo wrote about NATO? The Soviet Union collapsed, the Warsaw Pact dissolved, communist Russia became capitalist Russia and NATO expanded and gobbled up the former Warsaw Pact states and pushed itself to the Russian border (having told the Russians they would not do that if they disbanded the Warsaw Pact). Point 6 remains valid and is the real source of the military strife going on in Ukraine at the time of this writing. The rest of the discussion on flipping the military is, while interesting, basically out of date as it is predicated on the ideals of peaceful co-existence with the Soviet Union and a new world order based on this. This is, for Carrillo, still very iffy as the balance of power keeping the peace is also resting on nuclear weapons. This remains true today and the US is fostering international tensions over Russia, Korea, and China, as well as several countries in Latin America and with Cuba. NATO interventions at the behest of the US in the Balkans, Eastern Europe, Libya, Afghanistan and Iraq have been lugubrious.

NATO remains the main enemy of the peace and socialist movements. The question today is, if CPs take ministerial roles in countries who are members of NATO are they undermining Marxism-Leninism and becoming revisionist in the Menshevik sense and/or the Bernstein/Kautsky sense? The same question applies to the US with regard to de facto support for the Democrats in an uncritical manner and with the notion of not making vanguard demands that might upset the Center which supports the racist

29

imperialist practices of the Democratic Party. These are crucial questions of principle which Marxist-Leninists must continually debate and reassess as the revolutionary struggle progresses.

There are a few more pages in this chapter on Carrillo's views on how to win over the Army to tolerate a peaceful socialist electoral victory, they are based on the ideas that in the near future European countries will be uniting for mutual defense in a world which has brought about general disarmament — not the world we actually live in which has increased military spending and armaments. Nevertheless, the question still remains, is a peaceful transition possible as long as the Army is controlled by the ruling class? How would the Jan. 6 attack on the Capitol have turned out if the Joint Chiefs of Staff in the Pentagon had been Trump supporters? Fortunately, the ruling class is fairly united in not supporting Trump at this time and even had the Democratic Party supporting Trump Republicans against "moderate" Republicans in the primaries, confident that Trump Republicans could not beat Democrats in the general election. We shall soon see if this was a good tactic or not.

Finally, in order to build a democratic coalition to lead to a socialist election victory the CPs practicing Eurocommunism (that is only the CPs in advanced developed capitalist states) must abandon out of date old Communist outlooks.

Point 7.) The struggle for a democratic state "presupposes the renunciation of the idea, in its traditional form, of a *worker's and peasants's State.*" [p. 76] This turns out to be a gratuitous point anyway as no advanced capitalist State has a peasantry. This point is a lead into the real point Carrillo wants to make.

Point 8.) "This [democratic] conception of the State also means giving up the ideas of a State apparatus that is a party apparatus, a State apparatus controlled by a party apparatus; it is a question of creating a State apparatus which at every moment faithfully obeys the people's elected representatives and which cannot be manipulated against the will of the people." [p.76]

This is a can of worms best left unopened. We are giving up Lenin for Rousseau. The will of the people is the general will in a socialist state, it is simple (let socialism be constructed) but in Carrillo's democratic state with CP does not have the leading role but is at best only *primer inter pares* and there will be a particular will associated with each and every other democratic party in the state including non-proletarian parties representing petty bourgeois interests even after the grand bourgeoisie has been eliminated. Carrillo's subtext here is that the whole of Marxist theory must be dumped because it holds that the working class controls the state by means of the working class party, the Communists, the creators of all wealth (except that of nature) and surplus value by which all live. This is the exploited class on which all others live and when it takes power there is no lower class under it which it exploits, exploitation ends and there is no need for parties anymore (political parties are representative of different classes). There is no sense for the socialists to democratically take over the State of the ruling class just to maintain it. The CP has to play the central and leading role in the revolution and the State because, while all the other parties are expressions of their particular wills, the proletarians are the bearers of the general will - the will to end exploitation and suffering, the will to socialism.

31

Carrillo ends his chapter on a realistic note as he knows the ruling class is unlikely to roll over and play dead after it loses an election to the socialists. Faced with a victory by Carrillo's new political grouping of forces the victory may not "be won solely through political action and democratic government measures; it can happen that at a given moment it may be necessary to reduce by *force* resistance by *force*; that is to say that the qualitative transformation of this apparatus may not be entirely peaceful and a democratic government may find itself confronted by an attempted coup." [p.76] So, the barricades are back. Our last point will be:

Point 9.) Go ahead and take on the opposition, but keep your powder dry.

Chapter Four: "The Model of Democratic Socialism"

The Approach to Economic Problems

Point 1.) The Eurocommunist approach to establishing socialism does not follow the traditional Marxist model: I.e., "it presupposes *the long-term coexistence of public and private forms, not property."* [p.77] It's a stage on the road to socialism which will also have broken the control by monopoly of the state and the private sector. At the same time, we will keep the advanced production forces created by the monopoly capitalist state. This would be a great trick if we could do it peacefully.

Point 2.) Rational and democratic planning will be used. The "new man" ["new person" is PC today] will be formed by our educational system which will intellectually enlighten the proletariat and other sectors of society, it will be free and also apply to "the children of the well to do." [p. 79] We will educate the children of the "well to do" to have a more collective consciousness. We have at least a two-tiered society on Carrillo's road. How likely are the "well to do" to peacefully give up their privileged economic position in the private sector to the creation of socialism Carrillo envisions?

Point 3.) This system still provides for the appropriation of surplus value from the working-class, but we can control it by taxation and interest rates. To be democratic we have to let the capitalists have their own political parties (not the monopoly capitalists). " This system, which will still be economically mixed, will translate itself into a political regime in which the owners will be able to organize themselves not only economically but also in a political party or parties representative of their interests; this will be one of the component parts of political and ideological pluralism."[p.80] Carrillo thinks that after the socialists come to power (the monopoly capitalists are out of the picture due to socialist educational and cultural work in the broadest sense) the workers and the remaining petty capitalists will still duke it out in elections which will eventually lead to the capitalists throwing in the towel because of their defeats and gradual adoption of the collective mentality. Half a century has passed since this was proposed, how close does this program even have to get off the ground? Monopoly capitalism is firmly entrenched throughout the world (with the exception of China and a few small countries) and shows no signs of changing its spots.

Soviet Thinking and the Democratic Road

33

In this section Carrillo seeks to show that his peaceful road to socialism is not a rejection of the Soviet Union, but an alternative based on the particular historical circumstances of the late 20th century. It is always iffy to base one's views on predicted future developments while at same time not being beware of the actual factors at work around you.

Point 4.) Carrillo makes the point that we should be thinking of a coming worldwide advance to socialism, but we can't use a one size fits all approach. What is the reality of the 1970s? The reality is that despite its apparent strength and power, imperialism "has been disestablished, first of all by the Great October Socialist Revolution, then by the advance of socialism ….in Europe, Asia, Latin America, and through the whole process of decolonization." [p. 82] In hindsight we see this is not what was going on. The Great October Socialist Revolution was only 15 years away from being reversed and the return of capitalism established throughout the former Soviet Union, the advance of socialism in Europe was reversed and all the European socialist states were overthrown and also reverted to capitalism. In Asia socialism held on in North Korea and China and won a tremendous victory by the defeat and rout of US imperialism by the Vietnamese masses. In Latin America, Cuba remains the only socialist state that weathered the collapse of the Soviet revolutionary project and its worldwide aftereffects. Nicaragua and Venezuela are still in the process of experimenting with socialist ideas and we will have to wait and see what results.

If the Soviet Union and the advance of socialism was to be the backdrop which would ensure the peaceful road

34

to socialism in the developed capitalist world, then Eurocommunism was being built on quicksand. Nevertheless, Carrillo makes some valid points in this section which may provide a lifeline for some aspects of the peaceful road to socialism. He refers to two quotes from Khrushchev's reports to the 20th Congress of the Soviet Communist Party. This Congress was famous for revealing the many crimes and violations of communist morality committed by the Stalin leadership (of which he was a part) that occurred during the construction of socialism in the USSR. Stalin's role is still under evaluation today since not only was a socialist state consolidated under his leadership, but the NAZI menace to the world was defeated by Soviet arms (80% of the NAZI army was directed against Russia leaving 20% to fight the US, the UK and the free French.)

The two quotes we are interested in are—1) Khrushchev quoting Lenin: "All nations will arrive at socialism — that is inevitable but not all will do so in exactly the same way, each will contribute something of its own in one or another form of democracy, one or another form of the dictatorship of the proletariat, one or another rate at which socialist transformations will be effected in the various aspects of social life." [p.84] And 2) Khrushchev himself said, regarding socialism coming about by parliamentary means: "[T]he present situation [1956] offers the working class in a number of capitalist countries a real opportunity to unite the overwhelming majority of the people under its leadership and to secure the transfer of the basic means of production into the hands of the people." [p.85] Well, this opportunity was muffed. Eight years later an inter-party coup overthrew Khrushchev and put the Soviet Union on a path that led to stagnation and eventual collapse.

35

The two quotes sound right even if the opportunities mentioned by Khrushchev are not so clear nowadays (in our country some leftists are fighting the Trump menace by going all out in support of a scion of the worst imperialist power in the world—Joe Biden). Carrillo also admits that the Lenin quote may have been touched up a bit as Communist leaders have a habit of taking his quotes out of context and dressing them up a bit to support their own views. Carrillo remarked that Lenin was well known for having doubts about bourgeois democracy and universal suffrage under capitalism. Be that as it may, as long as the socialists are not being persecuted and can participate in bourgeois elections it seems they should do so and shelve talk about violence, etc. for a rainy day.

A More Fundamental Assessment of Democracy

In this section Carrillo seeks to clear up some confusions regarding the concept of "democracy." He wants to modify Lenin's concept of democracy. He points out that in times of revolutionary struggle the fierce urgency of now can lead to overstatements and generalizations which need later amendments.

Point 5.) In the heat of the revolution, Lenin, at times was in some of his writings "making one-sided and excessive generalizations [p [p.87] which is done by almost all leaders subject to the pressure of rapidly changing events. Fighting against reformists, who always appeal to "democracy" as the answer to the impulse that is breaking out in revolutionary violence to overthrow the capitalist state. Lenin, according to Carrillo, identifies "democracy" with "State." That is, Lenin sees bourgeois democracy as a tool of the dictatorship of the bourgeoisie to beat down the workers. The revolution will overthrow the state which will eventually wither away along with the idea of "democracy" which is a form of State with one class exploiting another. This whole discussion rests on different concepts of the state. Carrillo gives examples of the word "democracy" as used in different ways when talking about primitive communism, Athens, Rome, under capitalism, under socialism, etc.

This misses Lenin's point, he thinks "democracy": is a State supported method and under capitalism it is used to support the bourgeoisie— when Lenin says "democracy" will be abolished he means that under socialism the state and its apparatuses, including state sponsored "democracy" will wither away as will class and the people will live in communal self-governing organizations. This will not be a "democracy" in the formal institutional sense we have today but a natural spontaneous way of living in a classless society. Carrillo is using the term in its present capitalist sense, and he wants to use bourgeois democracy to build a new kind of socialist democracy that is transitional along with his political struggle to flip the institutions of capitalist society to serve socialist ends. It is this type of peaceful new democracy struggle on the road to socialism that Carrillo thinks Lenin would have doubts about— a nonexistent people's democracy that would come into reality by the successes of Eurocommunism and then move on to socialism.

Changes in the Appraisal of Universal Suffrage

Carrillo points out that traditionally communists have not thought of universal suffrage as part of the main road to socialism This is because communist parties were born out of the Russian Revolution which brought the communists to power without universal suffrage. Also those advanced capitalist countries with large socialist parties and universal suffrage and parliamentary democracy all ended up with the socialists supporting WWI and their own governments. Finally, the fascists came to power in Italy and Germany both of which had universal suffrage. [Just to be PC— "universal suffrage" at this time meant "universal male suffrage" Women got the vote in Germany in 1918, after WWI, in Italy on the local level in 1925 (Mussolini) and universally in 1945].

Carrillo defends universal suffrage as one of the main means to the road to power. All communists support it but not all communists give it the major importance that Carrillo does. [Political power grows out of (a.) the barrel of a gun, (b) the ballot box, (c) both (d) it's complicated.] Carrillo supports it because he favors a peaceful, nonviolent transfer of power via parliamentary democracy in a multi-party State. The failures of universal suffrage were caused not by failures of the vote, but by the failure to unify the working class and the middle strata around the democratic anti-fascist struggle. Carrillo points out that Dimitrov recognized this.

Point 6.) The development of the Popular Front stresses the importance of building unity between the working class and other progressive forces in the middle strata and petty bourgeoisie. The Eurocommunists and other revisionists go beyond Dimitrov, however, by trying to include elements of the ruling class whose objection to the monopolists is based on their own interests not on an objection to the exploitation and injustices of the capitalist order or to fascism per se as opposed to their exclusion from power themselves.

Now we come to one of Carrillo's strongest arguments in favor of the Eurocommunist peaceful road to power. These arguments are also used by those parties who reject Eurocommunism from the right. They are based on Engel's views from the 1890s. They are to be found in his introduction to Karl Marx's The *Class Struggles in France 1848-1850.*

Carrillo says that Engels admits the experiences of the last 20 or so years (the 1870s-90s) have caused him to completely revise his views on the conduct of the revolutionary forces. From the time of the *Communist Manifesto* communists envisioned a revolution to be fighting in the streets, barricades, the armed workers taking on the State and overthrowing it— one class, the workers, fighting the big bourgeoisie with the other strata and classes looking on to see who won.

What has changed? The growth of the State and changes in the tactics of the military make it almost impossible for street fighters to confront and overcome the organized military power of the State. The workers can no longer hope to be a lone class fighting the State. They need allies from the other oppressed sectors of the population. Politically what has changed that can make this possible? In Germany universal adult male suffrage was introduced in 1867. This is Engels' starting point.

Engels calls this "universal suffrage" and by the 1890s the German workers had used it to build up a mass proletarian party with substantial power in the parliament— the Reichstag. By using this power, the workers have been

39

able to exercise authority over the other State institutions and apparatuses of the ruling class State. Was Engels an embryonic Eurocommunist or worse, a modern-day social democrat? We shall see.

This is how workers use voting according to Engels: "In election agitation it provided us with a means, second to none, of getting in touch with the mass off the people where they still stand aloof from us; of forcing all parties to defend their views and actions against our attacks before all the people; and further, it provided our representatives in the Reichstag with a platform from which they could speak to their opponents in parliament, and to the masses without, with quite another authority and freedom than in the press or at meetings…(intro to Marx)." A far cry from following the Center or other forms of tailism. Not being in a Reichstag it's up to our press to do this.

Engels pointed out that more was done by these legal methods than by illegal methods, rebellions, trying to form uprising, etc. Engels did not foresee WWI or the rise of fascism and the NAZIs but thought, like Carrillo, the working class party would grow and grow, slowing taking over the State institutions and winning over the masses until it came to power. "Until the decisive day." (Ibid.) This victory will happen if we stick with this democratic road and give up the utopian dream of street fighting and violence.

Engels had every reason to think that this was the way to go, considering his historic period in the late 19th century where he could see the advances of German social democracy and compare it to the fate of the Commune. Of course, Engels, as Carrillo, left open the possibility that the ruling class would resort to violence, but he too thought the socialist forces would have become strong enough to be unbeatable. The horrors of the 20th century put an end to these optimistic hopes.

After WWII, as hope springs eternal in the human breast, Carrillo has found solace in Engels' words. In the Europe of half a century ago he opined "The Europe of today the socialist forces can enter the government and come to power through universal suffrage and they will maintain themselves in a leading position in society if they are able to keep the confidence of the people through periodical elections." [p.95] We still have leaders today with these hopes and optimistic views. They have a little touch of Santiago in the night. Who is to gainsay them?

Socialist Criticism and Forms of Democratic Struggle

Point 7.) "It is a necessity and an obligation to *open up a breach,* to achieve a *real differentiation* between those who sincerely cherish the values of democracy and political liberalism and those for whom democracy and liberalism mean only the preservation of the property of State monopoly capital and its economic privileges." [p. 96] In other words a breach between the phony progressives and the real progressives. The phonies are the liberals, and so-called socialists who act progressive as long as the capitalist system is not called into question. When that happens, when capitalism is threatened, they turn their coats and "become fascists."

In the fight we are in now the two groups are mixed up and it is hard to tell the phonies from the real progressives. The same was true in Carrillo's day. There are critics on

41

the left and right of the former socialist countries, the USSR, and positions taken by the communist parties that they think are wrong. Are they phony or sincere? Carrillo said that serious critics, not slanderers, who are trying to improve the struggle and complain about "real or supposed mistakes" are not *ipso facto* being phony. We can all work together as long as we have honest motives. Discussions, critical or not, different viewpoints, and suggestions can lead to better understanding and stronger progressive movements. "The only thing that should be banished from a society that's profoundly democratic is terrorism and physical violence as an instrument of political action, and the use of libel and slander against individuals and groups." [p.98-99] This is always a sign of phoniness in both groups and leaders pretending to be "left." Bossiness is also a sign of being a phony.

If we are going to be able to capture the capitalist state apparatuses by means of democratic advances, we must make sure we don't end up working with the phony elements who will, in a crisis, side with the enemy against us. This is why in our time we have to be very careful with who we work and want in a Popular Front. It would appear that we don't want elements from the phony left, let alone the phony center, who will turn to reaction when the time comes to turn towards socialism. We can work on some issues with these people but not uncritically.

The Biden administration, for example, is a major part of the capitalist-imperialist system destroying the planet and preparing for a major world war in the future if the US domination of the international arena looks to be ending, even if by peaceful means of economic development. It is a major enemy of the American and world working-class and only phony liberals and leftists pretend otherwise. Yet it has potentially progressive elements within it that can be won over to the progressive side and we must try and do that by means of constructive criticism of the weakness and faults of the administration which can be improved and worked with, and also by pointing out its deadly over-all nature. Eurocommunism would try working with like-minded other strata along with the proletariat to form a movement "that unifies the interests and ideas of the broadest sections." [p. 99]

The Role of the Party and the New Political Formation

Point 8.) "The new ideas about the road to socialism in the developed countries allow certain diversifications with regard to the role and function of the Communist Party." What are these Eurocommunist innovations? The Party will no longer view itself as the only representative of the working people. It will agree that other working-class parties, even with different philosophical perspectives, can represent the working class and the struggle for socialism. Carrillo said must earn the status of vanguard by our actions. Carrillo thought the Communists could work together with other such parties in a multi-party state. We would still be, however, the vanguard party. "It continues to be the vanguard party, in as much as it truly embodies a creative Marxist attitude." [p.100]

But to be a vanguard others must also see us that way. Since other parties don't have our advanced outlook, they tend to participate in bourgeois politics as usual [nothing has changed in the 50 years since this was written!] We can't do this, according to Carrillo.

43

Point 9.) "If they're to keep their vanguard role, the communist parties must strictly carry out *a concrete analysis of concrete reality*, which at times means not only refraining from going with the stream, but swimming against it....Either we turn our role as a vanguard into a reality in that way, or else that role is reduced to an ideological fantasy which may serve to console us from time to time for our ineffectiveness." [p.100]. Well, those leftists in the US who uncritically support Biden's domestic policies and the Democrats as the best way to defeat the ultra-right (swimming with the stream) cannot be accused of being Eurocommunists.

Point 10.) This is a major revision point aimed at the heart of traditional Marxist theory. "The party recognizes that, outside collective political tasks, each member is master of his fate [or her] as regards everything affecting his preferences, intellectual or artistic inclinations, and his personal relations." [p.101] While it remains private and not public. So, this proposition is not earth shattering, but the next is, at least for Marxists, this is the real essence of point 10. When it comes to different scientific theories of reality, and views in the humanities on art and literature and philosophy, all sorts of different schools of thought should be allowed in Party publications. "The party as such does not pass judgement except on questions of revolutionary strategy and political tactics." [Ibid.] In other words, Marxism is a purely pragmatic and utilitarian political philosophy.

This has never been the view of any real Marxist. Marxism has, from the beginning, been a philosophical worldview based on the merger of Hegelian/Marxian dialectical logic and a materialist scientific world view which we call Dialectical Materialism— it is an all-encompassing philosophy which includes the humanities and the natural and social sciences, especially history (historical materialism). We do not believe the class struggle is confined to politics; it is in fact based on economics of which politics is a reflection. We believe the class struggle is manifested in all aspects of culture and especially today in bourgeois capitalist culture.

We do pass judgement on scientific and cultural schools of thought. We would not permit creationism, for example, to be taught along with, or in place of, Darwinism in the educational system. We also take a stand on so-called scientific theories that promote racism and the superiority of one "race" or "ethnic" group over another. We also recognize that cultural creations in art and literature, theatre, movies, etc. reflect the class struggle and can promote reactionary anti-working class ideologies which act at the expense of the humanistic values of equality and basic rights for all that Marxism stands to promote now and after the abolition of the bourgeois political order. Carrillo's point 10 is anathema to the worldview of Marxism-Leninism (AKA scientific socialism).

Point 10, however, is a foundation stone to what Carrillo called the *new political foundation* which he hoped Eurocommunism would bring about. This was a hodgepodge of all the political parties, different class forces, and organizations, which have broken with monopoly capitalism and will all work together in peace and harmony with each other for the greater good of all. Only this never came about because, besides having contradictions with monopoly capital, they had different goals and values to preserve which contradicted those of the other members of the hodgepodge and none of them thought the Communists

45

were the vanguard as each thought they had the best positions. The hodgepodge couldn't work.

Take an example from our own country. No socialists, especially Marxists, want to see the racist, crypto-fascist Republicans elected to office. The monopoly capitalist Democratic Party doesn't want them elected either. The Democratic Party also hates all forms of socialism and especially Marxism. You would have to be nuts to think you could form a *new political foundation* based on a coalition which included the progressive forces of the socialist and Marxist left and the imperialist Democratic Party. The first ones to laugh us out of court would be the Democratic leadership. Eurocommunism was a dream that could never have come to fruition. Some aspects, as we have noted, of their thought may still be relevant, but the basic foundation of their *new political reality* was smoke and mirrors.

Eurocommunism and Social Democracy

The difference between Eurocommunism and Social Democracy is that the SDs have abandoned the goal of replacing capitalism with socialism. Communists seek to eliminate state monopoly capitalism and replace it with socialism. SDs seek reforms of the capitalist system and seek not to overthrow the capitalist state but to administer it. Nevertheless, the Communists seek to dialogue with the SD and socialist parties the same way they dialogue with Christians.

Point 11.) Eurocommunism can work with the Social Democrats because the Communists seek to win all the progressive groups over to the convergence of the new political reality that will replace monopoly capitalism.

Carrillo saw this as a process illuminated by "the evolution which has led France to the Union of the Left." [p.104]

This left union turned out to be a disaster for the French Party, it teamed up with the Socialists as a minor party in a Socialist government. The Socialists undertook to shore up the capitalist system, the French party bled membership, quit the "union" and never regained the political strength they had in the past. To this day they still form left fronts with other parties in attempts to regain their former place. They did not really turn towards Eurocommunist ideas until after the fall of the Soviet Union in 1991, 15 years after Carrillo's book, this despite the fact that they, along with the Italian Party and the Spanish Party under Carrillo, are considered to be one of the three founding parties of the movement. They have recently dropped the hammer and sickle as the symbol on their membership cards. Eurocommunism hasn't done them much good.

Anyway, despite what Carrillo said about the Social Democrats, after the breakup of the Soviet Union most Communist Parties split, or dissolved, and the Eurocommunists basically became social democrats in practice. About a third of the Communist Party in the United States split off to form the Committees of Correspondence for Democracy and Socialism which does not practice democratic centralism and has Marxists and social democrats as members. After the death of long serving leader Gus Hall in 2000, the Communist Party veered to the right under Sam Webb and his successors having disbanded the YCL and suppressed its theoretical journal, *Political Affairs*. Efforts have recently begun to reconstitute the YCL. The future of the party is uncertain as it appears to have abandoned

47

an independent Marxist-Leninist analysis of the class struggle and is following the lead of centrist elements affiliated with the Democratic Party. Only time will tell if this analysis is correct.

The Context of Our Development

Eurocommunism aims to make whichever country it is in independent of both the USSR and the USA as the two dominant military blocks. Well, there is no more USSR and capitalist Russia and socialist China appear to be substituting for the enemies of the USA/NATO block. There is now only the USA military block. The context described by Carrillo is really moot. The whole point of Eurocommunism was for Communists to be able to develop outside the Soviet orbit within advanced capitalism and to ally with other progressive forces and evolve peacefully into socialism. With no more USSR there is no need for "Eurocommunism," although many of its ideas have been taken over by communists in the advanced capitalist states — especially the idea of peaceful evolution (refurbished Bernstein revisionism).

But how would Eurocommunism have brought about a peaceful evolution? Three conditions are needed: 1) the left forces need a common strategy (just that of the communists alone won't do) 2) the left forces must make common cause with the Third World esp. progressive democratic countries pursuing anti-imperialist goals. 3.) The left forces must strengthen economic relations with the European and Asian socialist states. Since there are no more European socialist states this means basically with China, Laos, Vietnam, and North Korea (DPRK). We can add Cuba to this mix. What this really means is China as it has replaced the USSR as the #2 superpower. This is the post-Eurocommunist world context. None of the post-Eurocommunist parties have fulfilled all three of these conditions. While some communist parties are anti-NATO *in doctrina* they support and work with governments or organizations that are *de facto* pro-NATO.

There is one other idea left over from Eurocommunism. That is a European defense arrangement independent of the USA and USSR. Today that means an independent EU military independent of NATO. The US is opposed to that idea — it considers it redundant, and it doesn't want a large military force independent of its control. Europe is to remain a satellite continent.

Chapter Five: "The Historical Roots of Eurocommunism"

The Popular Fronts in Europe as Antecedents of "Eurocommunism"

Point 1.) The following 10 points constitute the program of Eurocommunism. Although Eurocommunism is *per se* defunct, the CPs today adhering to similar ideas can be seen as inheritors of the Eurocommunist teachings.

    1-   Democracy is the Road to Socialism
    2-   A multi-party system
    3-   Parliaments and Representative Institutions
    4-   Universal Suffrage
    5-   Independent Unions (free of state or party control)
    6-   Freedom for the Opposition

    7-   Human Rights
    8-   Religious Freedom
    9-   Cultural, Scientific, and Artistic Freedom
    10-   Popular Participation in all the major
forms off social activity

This is combined with independence from any international centers [No more automatic echoes of Soviet policies, or Chinese for that matter]. These 10 points are domestic, there are also 7 international points which constitute the Eurocommunist versions of "proletarian internationalism."

    1-   Cooperation and Peaceful Coexistence
    2-   No Military Blocks
    3-   No Foreign Military Bases
    4-   No Nuclear Weapons
    5-   Disarmament
    6-   Non-interference in the affairs of other countries
    7-   Self-determination for All Peoples

These positions did not spring up overnight. They have roots going back to the days of the Popular Front, but three major historical events have brought them to the forefront of Communist consciousness and discussion today [the 1970s] but even now they still reverberate:

    1-   The 20th Congress of the Communist Party
of the Soviet Union
    2-   The invasion of Czechoslovakia (1968)
    3-   The Sino-Soviet Split

The rest of this section is taken up by historical speculation on the part of Carrillo. In the political struggles of the 30s against fascism and Nazism, especially the Spanish Civil War and WW2, Carrillo was a major leader and knew most of the other Communist leaders. Behind the facade of a united Third International position on all the major issues, Carrillo points out the real internal disputes between the leadership of major Communist parties (the French, Spanish, Italian, British which wanted to tailor responses to fascism to their national features (to actually participate in Popular Front governments, or to remain outside of the government, for example.)

The Third International (directed from Moscow) position always won out and for unity the national CPs went along. The French party did not join the popular front government for example. Well, the fascists were on a roll, came to power, wiped out the CPs public presence, they went underground and didn't surface publicly until Germany was defeated by the USSR. Carrillo speculates that the fascists might have been halted if the Third International had not enforced its policies regardless of the different existential circumstances of the national CPs in Europe, etc. This is could've, would've, should've Marxism so I will skip it and go to the section where Carrillo was actually participating in one of these struggles — the struggle in Spain where he had firsthand knowledge.

The Spanish Experience - The Case of Trotsky

This is Carrillo's position in brief. When Spain became a Republic in the 1930s the CP was small and sectarian and following the line of the Communist International. It proclaimed a class war against the bourgeoisie— this was

51

class against class and no cooperation was allowed with the petty bourgeoisie or other classes— the workers would duke it out alone with the capitalists. The CP leaders however began to work with other left forces to broaden their appeal. These were pre-popular front days but there were changes under way in the International which facilitated these moves by the CP (this was 1933).

Soon the Popular Front was the new International position and it was in full swing in Spain. The CP also included the Trotskyists into the Popular Front and in the Front's government in Catalonia. This was non-sectarian at a time when communist parties around the world were fighting with Trotskyists. The collaboration did not last long, however, and the CP adopted the view of the International (the Soviet view) of Trotsky as an enemy of the Soviet Union.

Now, in the 1970s, Carrillo said, the communists are talking about Trotsky and the Trotskyist role in the civil war again— a reevaluation seems in order. In the 1930s people were unjustly accused of being "fascist agents." They are due for rehabilitation. Even nowadays in the 21st century there is much disinformation about this subject in circulation. In those days, Carrillo said, we Communists really believed that Trotsky and the Trotskyists were working for the fascists. A lot of this information was also being peddled by anti-communists as well.

The Moscow trials and the confessions of the accused persuaded the CP, as well as others, of Trotsky's guilt. But, Carrillo stresses, none of them in those days had any idea "of the infernal machine by means of which those confessions were obtained" [p.117]. The victims of the Moscow trials and the Trotskyists proclaimed their innocence and the Trotskyists tried to expose the methods by which confessions were coerced but we chose to believe the Soviet Union. Fascism was on the rise. The Soviet Union was the first and only socialist state and Stalin was its leader. We had no firsthand knowledge so, by "an act of faith," we believed what the Soviets told them. So, "it was possible for the myth that Trotsky was linked with the Nazis and was protected by American imperialism to arise and establish itself, and we youngsters of that period swallowed the official accounts of the October Revolution and of the subsequent civil war, in which Trotsky's role was passed over in silence." [p.117]

It is high time this myth be put to bed and an objective scientific account of Trotsky be written showing that Trotskyism was a trend within the Revolutionary Russian tradition instead of just treating it as some sort of pro-Nazi movement. Having said this, Carrillo notes "Trotsky's opinions on the Spanish Revolution of 1936-39 could not have been more profoundly mistaken."[p.118]

This is because he looked at Spain through the lens of the Russian Revolution and its tactics ignoring the fact that Spanish conditions were totally unlike the conditions facing the Bolsheviks.

Finally, the case of Andreu Nin is discussed. Andreu Nin was a Trotskyist leader of the POUM party during the Spanish civil war. He disappeared in questionable circumstances and it was alleged he defected to the fascists (Franco) or that he was murdered by the Communists depending on your views of the POUM. Carrillo said, after he did all he could to find out what happened, that Nin did not defect to the fascists and that he was indeed extra judicially murdered but that it was not done under the auspices of the CP —but members on their own may have been involved. The POUM was foiled in a coup attempt against the Republic during the civil war — this was an

53

act of high treason but Nin should have had his day in court.

The Spanish Experience: The popular Front

The leadership of the Spanish Republic in the early 1930s was in the hands of the bourgeois liberals. There had been cooperation between the socialists and liberals from 1931 to 1933. In 1934 the liberals alone were running the show. A real fascist threat developed and the socialist led Popular Front declined to work with bourgeois elements (the liberals). Seeing this disunity the fascists began an uprising, a civil war that lasted three years and brought Franco to power. The Popular Front joined with liberals when they saw what was transpiring, but by then it was too late, the war was underway.

Carrillo maintains that in the Republican held areas a unique sort of Popular Front came to be, unlike the other European Popular Fronts, and it foreshadowed the kind of new democracy that Carrillo thought must be transitional between bourgeois democracy and socialism which was the basis, later, for Eurocommunism. The closest analogy I can think of is that Carrillo's Republican zones were practicing a sort of participatory democracy à la 1960s SDS style.

"At that time we communists were already upholding the parliamentary democratic Republic, the representative bodies of the nationalities, which brought down on us a lot of criticism from leftists. Already at that time we thought that by maintaining these forms of representative democracy, by doing the same with the bodies of the nationalities, with local government bodies, and by developing forms of direct democracy in the factories and other enterprises, by giving the working people a direct say in the running of affairs at all levels, the foundations could be laid for a democracy of a new type which would proceed to socialism." [p.123] He also quotes from a letter he got from Stalin et. al., "It is very possible that the parliamentary road may turn out to be a more effective procedure for revolutionary development in Spain-than-it-was-in-Russia."-[p.124]

Despite subsequent revelations about Stalin, this letter shows that many Communists were seriously thinking about the parliamentary road being sometimes possible and this view was also backed by the 20th Congress of the CP of the Soviet Union. It is perhaps impolitic to point out a little over 30 years after this Congress the parliamentary road more often resulted in CPs being voted out of power than into power.

Here we might make a comment about the use of slates. Some CPs use slates to elect their leadership and claim this is what unions do. It is correct that unions opposed to democratic elections do this. This is what Carrillo says: "We communists always fought for the democratic election of factory committees, coming out against the unfortunately dominant attitudes which left the composition of those committees to nomination from above by the trade union bureaucracies." [p. 126] It is really ingenuous to claim that the use of slates is a democratic procedure.

Finally, Carrillo concludes, "it is not only from a Marxist analysis of present-day reality, but also from our own complex experience, that we derive the arguments in favor of the democratic socialism we advocate for our country." [p.129] It isn't too far off the mark to say that the arguments for Eurocommunism have not been fruitful.

55

The European Communist Parties After the Second World War

At the end of WWII, the CPs were at the height of their power. They had played the leading roles in the various underground resistance movements to Hitler and the Soviet Union had played the major role in the defeat of Hitler. They participated in the governments of the newly freed Western Europeans governments (Italy, France, and others) and they played by the rules of parliamentary democracy. They were so strong that had the Soviet Union told them to, they probably could have taken over these countries by force. The Soviet Union did not tell them to take power. Probably due to the Yalta agreement between Stalin and Truman. The Eastern European countries along the Soviet border occupied by the Red Army would become part of the Soviet sphere of influence, Western Europe of the American. Nevertheless, these CPs played by the rules of democracy by their own choices as well, even after 1947 when the Americans began the Cold War and the Communists were kicked out of the coalition governments.

Carrillo says another factor at work was trying to get free from Soviet control. Stalin had dissolved the Third International at the beginning of WWII (to show good faith to the Americans as allies against Hitler). Without the International the other CPs were no longer bound to the Communist Party of the Soviet Union. Yet they felt a loyalty towards the first socialist state. In 1947, after the Cold War began, Stalin founded the Cominform (Communist and Workers Parties Information Bureau) which brought the CPs together again under the guidance of the CPSU.

Democratic methods remained in force in the Western parties. This remained the case until 1956 when the Cominform was dissolved during the de-Stalinization process.

The Communist Party Spain operated under the principle that in Spanish affairs they had the final say and it was in international affairs that they followed the Soviet Union. The SU often did things on their own without consulting the other members of the Cominform and the others all went along for fear of being "excommunicated." An unforgivable error, according to Carrillo, was going along with the SU when it denounced Tito and condemned Yugoslavia when it showed signs of independence from Moscow.

For the Spanish party the "culminating" point was the Soviet led Warsaw Pact invasion of Czechoslovakia in 1968. No prior consultation, just the SU announcing the invasion to prevent capitalist restoration (with no proof) using the same methods as in the 1936 Moscow trials and the condemnation Yugoslavia— I.e., lies, disinformation, and stories "that were light years away from the truth." [p.132].

This is the background which led to Eurocommunism and a commitment to the peaceful democratic road to socialism and the independence of national CPs. Still, the Eurocommunists consider the Soviets comrades and fully support their struggle against US imperialism.

The Role of Violence in History

Carrillo tells us that the long years of the struggle against fascism has made communists more appreciative of (bourgeois) democracy and to support it in capitalist regimes, and also aware of its weak and under-appreciated

57

use in the socialist states. Nevertheless, communists will not abandon the revolutionary struggle to overthrow imperialism and capitalism throughout the world. It is not a struggle in this or that country but an international struggle to overcome the economic system of capitalism. Each country has its own struggle but we are all together in the hopes for this international elimination of the capitalist system.

For Carrillo, this is NOT a turn to social democracy and communists are not social democrats. We are not abandoning the possibility of a revolution. Should the capitalist block the democratic road to socialism and revolutionary alternatives appeared we would support the revolutionary overthrow of the capitalists. However, in Spain and countries in similar circumstances, the Eurocommunists declare the conditions have already arrived by which the nonviolent democratic electoral road is possible and that is how we will proceed to socialism. [40 years later in the 2000s we will find Carrillo not only no longer in the Communist Party but also a social democrat. He died in his 90s in 2012. So far, the "peaceful road to socialism" has always led to a similar destination, but that doesn't mean we won't find a fork in the road that gets us where we want to go.]

We are not turning our backs on the historic role of violence in history. Without the English Revolution (Cromwell), the American Revolution, the Great French Revolution, the wars of Napoleon, the bourgeoisie would never have been able to overthrow the feudal system and spread the capitalist system around the world and become the new ruling class. Political power did indeed grow from the barrel of a gun.

As far as today is concerned, the example of the Paris Commune energized the working class and spread the ideas of working class democracy— and the fact that we today have such advanced democratic rights in many countries is due to the response to the Russian Revolution and the defeat of Hitler and fascism for which the main credit goes to the Soviet Union and the Red Army which knocked out 80% of Hitler's military and ended the possibility of a German victory in WWII. The violence of the past is responsible for all this. But, Carrillo believes, this has also brought about a qualitative change in history where violence is no longer necessary. [Well, the Soviet Union and the Red Army are history and fascism is making a comeback so perhaps Carrillo's 'qualitative change' was just an illusion.]

The Russian Communists had no Choice in 1917 but to Take Power

Carrillo points out that Marx and Engels lived at a time when the working class was really only developed in parts of Western Europe and the U.S., England and France especially. Imperialism was just beginning (finance capital). Capitalism was fully developed and in its highest stages by the time of Lenin. Until WWI the three great international leaders of the working class were Marx, Engels, and then Kautsky. Kautsky's *Road to Power* was the go-to book for the revolutionary movement. The original "revisionist," Bernstein had published his book also (*Evolutionary Socialism*) but it was "unorthodox."

The official theory was more or less as follows: Capitalism was going to fall apart due to internal contradictions after it had fully developed the productive forces to their
59

maximum and this would happen in the most advanced capitalist countries where the class-conscious Marxist workers would take over and begin the construction of socialism. The rigors of WWI brought about the collapse of capitalism in backwards Russia, socialism would be impossible there, what was needed was a bourgeois government that would bring Russia into the world of advanced capitalism before socialism would be possible.

Socialists saw WWI coming and argued about the possibility of a revolution breaking out in countries as a result. The consensus was that if it did in a backwards area it could be successful because the revolution in the advanced countries would come to its aid. This is similar, e.g., to the Soviet Union coming to the aid of the Cuban Revolution which allowed it to survive the U.S. while it consolidated itself. This didn't work in Afghanistan. The Bolsheviks were forced to take power in Russia because the country was falling apart and the provisional bourgeois government was totally incompetent. The Bolsheviks ended up isolated in a backward country and the revolution didn't happen in the advanced countries. After waiting for the revolution for 10 years Stalin came to power and proclaimed "Socialism In One Country"— they tried for about 70 years but that whole system finally caved in. Neither the Eurocommunists nor the anti-Eurocommunists saw this coming.

But Carrillo did see all the problems, as well as the good things, that "Stalinism" brought about. Industrialization, economic development, scientific advance (Sputnik) but at the expense of democracy, free expression, and lower living standards than the West. His final views were that, for backward areas (underdeveloped) violent Revolution may be required and should be supported (Cuba, Vietnam, Laos, Korea, China) but in the advanced capitalist countries the road to power was the democratic parliamentary road towards a peaceful arrival at socialism. For all that, however, Carrillo says the Communists of today are the children of the great Russian Revolution and of the CPSU and the whole history of our movement. We are not Social Democrats who have always opposed the revolutionary forces and seek to merely reform, not do away with capitalist oppression and exploitation.

Chapter Six: The Dictatorship of The Proletariat

Carrillo wants to give up this concept. His reasons are basically related to those expressed a few years ago in an article in *Political Affairs.net* on the ten worst and best ideas in Marxism, written by Joe Sims. It is the number one worst idea: "1. "Dictatorship of the proletariat." Probably the worst phrase uttered by a political theorist ever. Who wants to live in a dictatorship? Even if I agreed with it conceptually, (which I don't), the Machiavellian in me has enough sense not to repeat it. Indefensible. And by the way, working-class "hegemony" (whatever the hell that means, sorry Gramscians), isn't much better."[1]

Carrillo writes: "The term *dictatorship* has in itself become hateful in the course of the present [20th] century,

---

[1] Joe Sims, "This Week's Ten Worst and Best of Marxism," *Political Affairs* (August 15, 2008): https://paeditorsblog.blogspot.com/2008/08/this-weeks-ten-worst-and-best-of.html

which has seen the most abominable fascist and reactionary dictatorships, among them Franco, and has known the
crimes of Stalinism— that is to say, the phenomenon aris-
ing from the corruption of the dictatorship of the proletariat — and the evils of totalitarianism of one sort or another; all that is enough to justify the abandonment of the
political use of the term." Who indeed wants to live in a
dictatorship?

Carrillo sees a problem. It is pragmatic and practical to
abandon the term in our cadre work, but what about Marxist theory? Marx, Engels, and Lenin used the expression
and thought it was a cornerstone of Marxist theory. In the
following, Carrillo will deal with this conundrum.

Marx and Engels on the State

In the *Communist Manifesto*, Carrillo says, Marx and
Engels for the first time conclude that the State's main pur-
pose is "for the domination of one class over another."
[p.145] This is still true today, in Spain or the US, it makes
no difference. "Even in countries where there are the most
liberties, the State is the organized power of one class for
oppressing another."

Fascism is the worst State form the ruling class uses to
oppress the working class and working people in general.
Communists understand that the bourgeois democratic
State is also a tool of oppression against the workers
but we do not dismiss bourgeois democracy as having no re-
deeming values. The rights and liberties found in democratic states are the result of the major and minor victories
in the class struggle that the workers have won over the
years. The bourgeoisie instituted rights for itself as against
the feudal and monarchist regimes it took power from and

working-class struggles have expanded those rights to cover its class as well as it could.

Carrillo continues by saying Marx & Engels in the *Manifesto* and later works equated *"the raising of the proletariat to the position of ruling class* with *winning the battle of democracy."* [p.147]

We should note that if we win the battle for democracy and become the ruling class, we will have to oppress another class (that is what the State is for) i.e., the bourgeoisie. Traditionally this has been called the *democratic dictatorship of the proletariat.* A term not used by Carrillo. Why "democratic dictatorship"? Because for the first time in history the ruling class will represent the interests of the vast majority of the people, will be the working people themselves taking control of the economic foundations of society and the State as such will begin to cease to exist with the elimination of the bourgeoisie, there being no class left to oppress, the State will "wither away."

The question is— Can this be done peacefully under the ground rules of bourgeois democracy? Will the present capitalist ruling class allow a peaceful transition? Carrillo's answer is "Yes"— this can happen in the advanced fully developed capitalist countries because the revolutionary forces will have convinced all the various class interests and organizations that socialism is the best of all possible worlds by means of purely democratic struggle and the capitalist ruling class will realize that resistance is futile. But this has never happened, you say "Don't be such a negative Nellie!" "Things do not have to be always the same and in the end they are certainly not always the same, even though in particular historical conditions they may have been so." [p.149]

63

Why the Concept of the Dictatorship of the Proletariat?

In the days of Marx, Engels and Lenin (MEL) the proletariat did not amount to a majority of the population so if a revolution broke out that brought the workers to power, they had to impose the dictatorship of the proletariat to maintain themselves in power during the transition to socialism. MEL were aware that not being in the majority, the dictatorship was necessary. This is Carrillo's position. But Lenin, aware of the fact that the vast majority of Russians were in fact peasants, i.e., petty bourgeois in Marxist terms, used the slogan "Dictatorship of the Proletariat and the Peasantry." So, this was a democratic majority and still a "dictatorship" to repress the capitalists as a class. However, the country was underdeveloped.

Carrillo does not want to dismiss the writings of MEL on the necessity of the dictatorship of the proletariat — *for their historic period*. His position is that in the modern world of the highly developed capitalism of Europe and the USA plus a few other highly advanced economies the traditions of bourgeois democracy are so ingrained that the transition to socialism can take place without the need for the dictatorship of the proletariat. Well, these traditions are so ingrained that, in the USA, we just had an election (2020) which the defeated sitting president tried to declare rigged and that he won it. Had he succeeded in remaining in power there would be no question about the validity of the dictatorship of the proletariat still being on the venue even in so called advanced democracies.

If Carrillo is correct, and the concept of a dictatorship of the proletariat is no longer politically relevant for advanced capitalist states, it is not the case that the concept of the "hegemony" of the working class in the transitional state is outmoded. The working class will be the leading class in this state because it has the most advanced ideas and is the only class that can actually bring about the socialist transition, but the other classes and strata in the state will follow the lead of the workers because of the good examples they set, not due to coercion.

Finally, there is the case of the Soviet Union and the Soviet model. The totalitarian state apparatus created by Stalin created a state that was not capitalist, was not bourgeois, but was a failed workers state because the workers were not the ones really controlling the state. It was controlled by an undemocratic bureaucratic caste and was unable to make a real advance towards socialism. There were good aspects and benefits provided to the people that they lacked in capitalist states but it was frozen in a stagnation that prevented it from further socialistic advances.

This whole issue is now moot. The Soviet Union imploded because it was unable to dialectically resolve the contradiction between its goal of socialism and its Stalinist power structure, which Khrushchev dented, but was unable to eliminate. The world communist movement is now on its own. The parties in the advanced capitalist countries must work out their own salvation— Lenin's ideas are still the best ones for them to consult, but many parties only give lip service to Marxism-Leninism. The Chinese experiment is still in progress and world imperialism, led by the US, will do anything it can to see that it fails. It is in the interests of all communists, socialists, and genuine progressives to see that it doesn't.

What Type of State

Carrillo points out that MEL saw two stages of the revolution— the first, Socialism, creates the working class led state, eliminates all exploiting classes, and then evolves into the second and final stage, Communism, a classless society free of human exploitation.

Carrillo says that the real world is quite unlike this ideal of how the revolution will turn out. While real social advances have been made in the USSR and the Eastern European socialist countries, they are still backward in the area of consumer goods due to the legacy of destruction of WWII and their backward starting points compared to the advanced Western countries. Unfortunately, the CPs in these countries have taken to talking about socialism as if they are already at that stage and freedom to argue about this with the authorities is restricted and forbidden.

This has alienated large numbers of ordinary citizens who see the freedoms allowed in the Western democracies and become skeptical and disillusioned regarding real socialism because they are told the transitional phase, still full of backward capitalist manifestations and practices, *is* socialism.

Carrillo says the people will eventually move to replace the *status quo* and he fears "they will throw out the baby with the bathwater" - i.e., because the bureaucratic CPs will not lead the reform movements correctly, the people will abandon the goal of socialism. [p.161] Carrillo's worries seem to have been correct. This happened in the socialist bloc. But in the Soviet Union it was the CP itself, in its top leadership, that "lost the faith." Carrillo thinks the democratic measures advocated by Eurocommunism will prevent this from happening during the revolutionary transformation to come in Western Europe, etc. [p.161]

This is what happened in the USSR. With the revolution in power with Lenin as its leader the masses were filled with enthusiasm for building socialism. The USSR did not have an advanced capitalist infrastructure. It had not gone through the state of advanced capital accumulation needed for such an infrastructure. Socialism needs to grow out of that already existing infrastructure. "[N]o account was taken of the fact that the new State might find itself compelled to carry out, before anything else, a *typically capitalist* task ... the content of which did not undergo a fundamental change just because it was given the name 'socialist accumulation.'" [p.162]

To make a long story short, that 'accumulation' was sweated out of the Soviet population and it was carried out under the direction of a state bureaucracy composed of the most class consciousness and dedicated workers who directed a mass population in which that consciousness did not yet exist and which it tried to imbue with that consciousness. This was a dictatorship of the party over the proletariat. The growth of Soviet industry + the patriotic sentiments unleashed by the NAZI invasion and defeat accounts for the popularity of Stalin despite the excesses, and abuses, and crimes committed during this period. Carrillo also notes that there were tremendous economic, cultural, and even spiritual advances also made at that time based on true revolutionary energy and sacrifices — so it is wrong to only dwell on the misdeeds of this era and fail to accentuate the positive. But we no longer need Stalinism as a model where there is a regime of bourgeois democracy in place which we can use. Stalinism was a revolutionary technique, which ultimately failed, designed for a backward underdeveloped country that lacked the real-world objective economic materialist

67

infrastructure to grow upon and make a transition to socialism.

Was failure inevitable? Carrillo did not think so. It was possible, at least in theory, to have democratized the system and prevented the collapse. We know that that didn't happen because Khrushchev's successors closed down "the thaw" he initiated. In the 1970s Carrillo still hoped the Soviet system would self-correct and become again a model for others. "[P]erhaps what is lacking is the political analysis of the system which Khrushchev was unable to make or did not know how to make at the Twentieth Congress and which could be the starting point for a new leap forward on the part of the Soviet Union and all the socialist countries." [p.165] After Khrushchev came the Brezhnev era of stagnation and then *après Brejnev le déluge.*

The World Environment and its Influence on the State

In this last part of the chapter Carrillo seeks to explain why socialism went off the tracks in the Soviet Union. No one, friend or foe of the Soviet Union, least of all Carrillo, would have guessed that in less than fifteen years the Soviet Union would be history and capitalism was being restored in Russia.

Born in the midst of WWI, suffering through three years of a brutal civil war, surrounded by imperialist powers planning its overthrow, the revolutionary government, after the founding of the USSR in 1922, realized it could not survive without rapid industrialization and centralization of power. Lenin and the Bolshevik leaders did not think the revolution could survive without being aided by a revolution in the advanced capitalist world which would come to its assistance. This didn't happen and the Soviet Union was an orphan. The State that developed could not have survived had it been committed to the kind of Western style bourgeois democracy that Carrillo supported which, in fact, didn't really come into its own until after WWII. The existential parameters in which the young Soviet state found itself situated "confirmed the impossibility of building *complete socialism* in a single country without socialism also triumphing in a series of developed countries." [p.166]

The system created by Stalin enabled the Soviet Union to industrialize and repel the Nazi invasion in WWII and the Red Army captured Berlin in 1945. The Soviet Union was a non-capitalist state run for the material benefit of working people by an authoritarian communist party which prevented the development of a worker's democracy due to the top-down vertical structure of the devolution of power from the leadership of the CPSU to the lower levels of the party and from thence to the populace at large. It was supposed to be a democratic centralist party but it was centralist without the democratic element. It was flawed but still there was no capitalist exploitation of the working class and a different international environment would have allowed its democratic and socialist potentials to manifest themselves. Think of what the Cubans could have accomplished, and be accomplishing, without the US blockade smothering their potentials.

The Soviet model was imposed on the new Socialist Bloc of counties that emerged in Eastern Europe after WWII. The exception was Yugoslavia, which developed its own model. This was the result of the Cold War initiated by the US — the Soviet Union had to hunker down to protect itself and the allied Socialist bloc was governed by

69

Soviet allied parties that had looked to it for leadership against Hitler and the NAZIS and for the struggle against US imperialism and now followed its lead in both domestic and international affairs. The need for a common defense and the use of social income to build up the military rather than to enhance consumer goods availability hindered any developments favorable to democratic pluralism and reenforced the vertical structure of governance in the socialist bloc. Writing in the late 1970s, Carrillo concluded, "The context in which the global confrontation presents itself today does not favor the transformation of the Soviet Union into a state of working-class democracy." [p.168]

Carrillo sees a problem with the Soviet leadership. They fail to see that their model is flawed due to the unfavorable historical circumstances that they have faced in trying to construct socialism over the last half century. [They were in fact 15 years away from collapse]. They were claiming to already have achieved socialism and were about to enter the communist stage. The CPs around the world were supposed to follow this line and hitch their own parties to the fate of the Soviet Union in the Cold War which we were told we were winning due to the general crisis of capitalism. But the leaders of major CPs in Europe, especially in Italy, Spain and France didn't see it that way. They saw socialism as an expansion of democracy while in the Soviet block it was limited and subject to over determination by party censorship. They didn't see "proletarian internationalism" as simply as uncritically following the Soviet line.

"We in the communist parties which are functioning in the capitalist countries cannot accept the idea that the victory of socialism is determined in the confrontation between the countries in which capitalists no longer exist and those which still preserve capitalism."[p.169] This is one of the signature positions of Eurocommunism. Many CPs around the world rejected this movement and remained allied ideologically with the Soviet Union, including the party in the US, all were caught flat footed with the collapse of the Eastern bloc. Some CPs dissolved, others became social democratic in name or *de facto* programmatically. Eurocommunism as a distinct movement disappeared but some parties formally anti-Eurocommunist, including in the US, more or less adopted the Eurocommunist outlook— peaceful electoral transition, pluralism (multi-party democracy), rejection of the dictatorship of the proletariat, etc.

Carrillo ends his book with the hope that as Eurocommunism grows in the West it will help the Soviet Union transform "into a real working people's democracy." [172]

After the Czech comrades were put down in 1968 by the Warsaw Pact, Brezhnev sitting in the Kremlin may have heard the death knell of Czech reform. If he had asked for whom the bell tolls, he would not have liked the reply.

71

9 780578 275857